New York Revisited

Most of the illustrations in this edition were reproduced from original photographs and drawings which appeared in *Harper's Weekly, Harper's Monthly Magazine*, and *Harper's New Monthly Magazine*. Also included are illustrations from the Collection of the New-York Historical Society and from the New York Public Library Picture Collection.

The jacket illustration is from a painting by John Edwin Jackson, which appeared in *Harper's Monthly Magazine*, August 1907.

The interior text type is 14-point Cochin. This edition was specially printed on 60-pound Liberty Antique.

New York Revisited

ê

Henry James

With an introduction by Lewis H. Lapham

FRANKLIN
SQUARE
P·R·E·S·S

New York

Published by Franklin Square Press, a division of
Harper's Magazine, 666 Broadway, New York, N.Y. 10012.

First edition.

First printing 1994.

Library of Congress Cataloging-in-Publication Data

James, Henry, 1843-1916.
New York revisited / by Henry James ; introduction by Lewis H.
Lapham.
p.cm.
ISBN 1-879957-14-0 : $14.95
1. New York (N.Y.) — Description and travel. I. Title.
F128.5.J24 1994
917.47'10441 — dc20
93-43414
CIP

Book and jacket design by Deborah Thomas.
Edited by Kathryn Belden.

Manufactured in the United States of America.

This book has been produced on acid-free paper.

Contents

Introduction

❧

Rattle of Gold

> Mammon, *n.* The god of the world's lead-
> ing religion. His chief temple is in the holy
> city of New York.
> —Ambrose Bierce,
> *The Devil's Dictionary* c. 1887

AFTER AN ABSENCE of more than twenty years, Henry James in the summer of 1904 returned to the United States to conduct a tour of lectures and renew his acquaintance with what he called "the huge American rattle of gold." He was sixty-one years old, at the high-water mark of his fame and in full possession of his literary faculties — and his reception in the grand tier of American society was as stately as his prose. He remained in the country for nearly a year, presenting himself in the persona of "the revisiting spirit," traveling in no small luxury and speaking

11

to appreciative audiences in cities as distant as Los Angeles and on topics as remote as "The Lesson of Balzac" and "The Question of Our Speech." Between engagements on the public stage, James stayed with friends, among them Edith Wharton (in Massachusetts) and Henry Adams (in Washington, D.C.), and gathered the notes and observations that he subsequently distilled into an anthology of impressions called *The American Scene.* Prior to its framing in the pages of that book, the essay on New York appeared in installments in *Harper's Monthly Magazine,* in the issues of February, March and May 1906. James already had composed stray sightings of the city taken over a period of months (between August 1904 and June 1905) into a dark and glaring portrait of Mammon. Both awed and frightened by "the terrible town," he saw nothing of the city's playfulness or wit, and his essay proceeds along the implacable lines of a painting by Hieronymus Bosch or a photograph of J. P. Morgan.

Nowhere in America was the rattle of gold more clearly seen or easily heard than on the island of Manhattan at the zenith of the Gilded Age, and if James's essay bears reading ninety years after it was first published, it is because the city still retains the character in which he described it—"expensively provisional," forbidden the pleasures of art or the comforts of history, oddly uncertain of itself despite the bluster of its immense wealth and sham refinement, willing to sell, at a steep discount and on an hour's notice, last week's priceless truth or yesterday's incomparable celebrity. To other observers, New York has shown itself in more flattering lights (I think of E. B. White's essays or the sketches of Walt Whitman and Washington Irving), but James means to confront Behemoth, and he perceives New York as the realized ideal of a society devoted to the worship of money—the annihilating spirit of finance capitalism achieving its most perfect expression not only as architecture but also as a social order and a style of feeling. He puts to the city the questions of the reproving moralist rather than those of the applauding journalist, and his essay stands in the line of spiritual objection that descends through the genealogy of American letters from the first sermons in the Puritan wilderness through the essays of Ralph Waldo Emerson, the epigrams of Ambrose Bierce, the theory of Thorstein Veblen, the novels of Edith Wharton and Theodore Dreiser.

The inferno into which James descended from the innocence of the English countryside was a New York excited by the violent banging and bellowing of a construction boom. Everywhere in the loud and narrow streets that to James's mind were arranged in an "inconceivably bourgeois scheme of composition," new office buildings, new town houses, new hotels jostled with one another for a place in the newly precious light and air north of 14th Street. With the completion that autumn of the New York Times Building on West 43rd Street, what had been known as Longacre Square became Times Square. The subway system opened in October, and Mayor George B. McClellan invited 15,000 citizens, all of them presumably damned but many of them wearing top hats, to ride the first uptown trains from City Hall to Broadway and West 145th Street. Workmen under the Hudson River completed the railroad tunnel joining the island of Manhattan to Jersey City and the American mainland, and in November Colonel Teddy Roosevelt, lately of the Rough Riders and the victory at San Juan Hill, captured the White House and promptly published plans and blueprints for building the Panama Canal. On the New York Stock Exchange, the Dow Jones industrials average approached the triumphant figure of 100, and 1,250 square feet of ground at No.1 Wall Street sold for $700,000, the highest price ever paid for any piece of real estate anywhere in the United States, or, to the best recollection of the press agents employed by William Randolph Hearst's *New York Journal-American*, anywhere in the world.

Then as now, the city's spoils were unevenly divided between the rich and the poor. The Hotel Astor opened with a bray of band music at about the same time that the Darlington Hotel collapsed under the weight of its faulty construction, killing a number of workers and convicting one of its owners of manslaughter. The immigrant swarm on the Lower East Side measured the density of its population at 1,000 people per acre, a ratio that exceeded the crowding in the slums of Bombay. Uptown among pillars of Italian marble, the city's captains of industry and princes of finance, known to the newspapers as "nature's noblemen," staged decorative costume balls, bought diamond collars for their dogs and feasted on oysters served in golden bowls. The names — Rockefeller, Vanderbilt, Harriman, Morgan, Mills, Gould — have since become synonymous with the divine origins of old American money, but in 1904 the fortunes were new, and J. D. Rockefeller was still enough of a bragging *arriviste* to say that by comparison with his own wealth, the riches of J. P. Morgan were those of "a pygmy."

The expensive names in the newspapers have changed, and most of the buildings have been replaced (if not three or four times, then at least once or twice), but the "play of wealth and energy and untutored liberty" remains much as it was in 1904, "half merry, half desperate," the breath of existence being "that of youth on the run . . . with the prize of the race in sight, and new landmarks crushing the old quite as violent children stamp on snails and caterpillars." Any reader wishing to look upon the dark side of the American moon has only to consult the volume in hand, which is why it still can start an argument, still propose a text for an editorial in *The Nation* or one of Pat Buchanan's campaign speeches. Open the essay on almost any page, and within the space of a paragraph James provides a vision of Hell:

On the despair of the populace:

> Speaking not least, for instance, of the way "the state of the streets" and the assault of the turbid air seemed all one with the look, the tramp, the whole quality and *allure*, the consummate monotonous commonness, of the pushing male crowd, moving in its dense mass—with the confusion carried to chaos for any intelligence, any perception; a welter of objects and sounds in which relief, detachment, dignity, meaning perished utterly and lost all rights.

On the ugliness of the architecture:

> The building can only afford lights, each light having a superlative value as an aid to the transaction of business and the conclusion of sharp bargains.

16

Doesn't it take in fact acres of window-glass to help even an expert New-Yorker to get the better of another expert one, or to see that the other expert doesn't get the better of *him*? It is easy to conceive that, after all, with this origin and nature stamped upon their foreheads, the last word of the mercenary monsters should not be their address to our sense of formal beauty.

On the emptiness of society:

The social question quite fills the air, in New York, for any spectator whose impressions at all follow themselves up; it wears, at any rate, in what I have called the upper reaches, the perpetual strange appearance as of Property perched high aloft and yet itself looking about, all ruefully, in the wonder of what it is exactly doing there.

No matter what the season, the perspective or the time of day, James sees in "the great face of New York" only those features and expressions that confirm his worst and fondest suspicions. Contemplating the skyline of lower Manhattan from a railroad barge in the Bay—the "revisiting spirit" is en route from Washington to Boston, keeping

17

company with his Pullman car as it is majestically towed
around the Battery—James gathers an impression of
"dauntless power," of a pitiless energy so vast in scale that
it shrivels the literary imagination, the city inhuman and
"steel-souled," busy with the work of "brandished arms
and hammering fists and opening and closing jaws. . . . an
enormous system of steam-shuttles or electric bobbins"
geared to the never-ending noise of coining money. Some
days later, walking on lower Broadway in the vicinity of
Wall Street, he is moved to a feeling of pity for the "caged
and dishonored condition" of Trinity Church, dwarfed by
the surrounding office buildings, sold into bondage by the
very church wardens charged with preserving its grace. In
Washington Place, James looks for the house in which he
was born in 1843 (when New York was made mostly of
brick, and chickens wandered the unpaved streets), but the
house has been torn down—obliterated, crushed, trampled
by "the heavy foot-prints . . . of a great commercial
democracy." Escaping the assault of the streets on a cold
afternoon in January 1905, James attempts the lobby of
the Waldorf-Astoria, then at 34th Street and Fifth Avenue,
and finds himself instantly embraced by the violent
"essence of the loud New York story." In alliance with the
expensive restaurants of the day (most notably Sherry's
and Delmonico's), the reception rooms at the Waldorf pro-

vided the showier elements of society with the settings in
which to admire themselves as jewels of great price, but
James, appalled by the vulgar splendor of the scene—pot-
ted palms, "innumerable huge-hatted ladies," bad violin
music, marble fountains, "a gorgeous golden blur"—
deplores the lack of hierarchy and decorum. He can't tell
the difference between the *demi-mondaines* and the women
of fashion or substantial family; among the gentlemen he
cannot distinguish the cardsharps from the bankers. In
England, where James had been living for more than thir-
ty years, one knew at a glance whether one was talking to
a jockey or a duke, but in America, in "the supremely gregarious state" that recognizes no value other than money,
the pervasive "social sameness" reduces all refinement of
feeling and graciousness of manner to the traffic in mere
publicity. James compares the effect to a circus exhibition,
or a dance performed by an army of puppets, a spectacle
so empty of human meaning that he withholds from the
personages assembled in the hotel lobby the rank and dignity of a personal pronoun:

> It sat there, it walked and talked, and ate and
> drank, and listened and danced to music, and oth-
> erwise revelled and roamed, and bought and sold,
> and came and went there, all on its own splendid

terms and with an encompassing material splendor, a wealth and variety of constituted picture and background, that might well feed it with the finest illusions about itself.

During the same month that James "looked briefly in" at the Waldorf, Edith Wharton published, in *Scribner's*, the first installment of *The House of Mirth*, a novel in which the heroine, a young and beautiful woman named Lily Bart, drifts like a precious ornament on the bright surface of the frivolous, albeit brutal, society summoned into existence by the riches of the Gilded Age. Wharton intended a bitter satire on the self-preoccupation of an ignorant plutocracy. Her heroine declines to sell herself as a commodity, and the novel shows her being inexorably forced out of the soft, well-lighted atmospheres of luxury, "the only climate she could breathe in," into the deserts of poverty. She cannot live in a world without carriages, engraved invitations, new dresses and the round of expensive amusements to which she had become accustomed. Unable to eat from broken china in the squalid part of town, she prefers to die rather than suffer "the humiliation of dinginess."

The House of Mirth addresses itself to what in 1905 was still a relatively small circle of people entranced by their reflections in a tradesman's mirror. Over the ninety years since Wharton published the novel and James beheld the "gilded labyrinth" of the Waldorf, the small circle has become considerably larger, and the corollary deformations of character show up in all ranks of American society, among all kinds of people caught up in the perpetual buying of their self-esteem.

In the equations of American failure and success, the values assigned to the words, "money" and "class," shift with the elevation of the social terrain, the tone of voice, the cost of the shrimp and the angle of the sales pitch. Few words come armed with so many meanings or as much ambivalence. Sometimes they serve as synonyms for freedom or beauty or truth, sometimes as surrogates for God. The profusion of meanings is peculiarly American. Among Europeans the two words refer to phenomena more or less concrete—to a store of wealth or an accident of birth, but with the Americans it isn't so simple. We impart spiritual connotations to the texts of money, and it is this transfer of value that troubles James. He was raised among the bleak moral precepts of Puritan New England, and having become accustomed to the class distinctions accepted by his European friends as acts of Providence, he cannot bear the fierce and shrieking story of self-invention, the insolent spectacle of upstart millionaires—crude fellows, illiterate and loud—striking the poses of nobility.

Like many Americans before and since, James cannot decide whether money is a virtue or a sin, and because it means so many things to him—spiritual as well as temporal—he is at a loss to know how to hold its majesty at bay.

Well before the American colonists declared their independence from Britain, they declared themselves of two minds about the dream of riches. The party of transcendence thought that money was merely a commodity, as drab as straw or as plain as wood, and that the American experiment was about the discovery of a moral commonwealth. The party of Mammon, equally zealous but not so pious, thought that money was a sacrament and that America was about the miracle of self-enrichment. The congenital enmity between these two temperaments gives rise to the argument that runs like a theme for trumpet and drums through the whole music of our history, literature and politics.

The *arriviste* theologians in Massachusetts Bay assumed that they had been granted what they called a "special appointment," and they knew that they would suffer the punishment of ecclesiastical foreclosure if they failed to make good on the deal and bungled the subdivision of the New Jerusalem. If America failed, the cosmos failed. Not only would the Americans have nowhere to go, but the whole scheme of salvation—the laws of nature, history and science, the ground of being; the rigging of human thought—all of it would come loose and blow away in the wind. Blessed by the prayers of Calvinist divines, the first American fortunes were founded on the slave trade and the traffic in bootleg rum.

The national distrust of the contemplative temperament proceeds less from an innate Philistinism than from a suspicion of anything that cannot be counted, stuffed, framed or mounted over the fireplace in the den. Men remain free to rise or fall in the world, and if they fail it must be because they willed it so. The visible signs of wealth testify to an inward state of grace, and without at least some of these talismans posted in one's house or on one's person, an American loses all hope of demonstrating to himself the theorem of his happiness. Seeing is believing, and if an American success is to count for anything in the world, it must be clothed in the raiment of property. As often as not it isn't the money itself that means anything; it is the use of money as the currency of the soul.

Against the faith in money, other men in other times and places have raised up countervailing faiths in family, honor, religion, intellect and social class. The merchant princes of medieval Europe would have looked upon the American devotion as sterile cupidity; the ancient Greeks would have regarded it as a form of insanity. Even now, in the last decade of a century commonly defined as American, a good many societies both in Europe and Asia manage to balance the desire for wealth against the other claims of the human spirit. An Englishman of modest means can remain more or less content with the distinction of an aristocratic name or the consolation of a flourishing garden; the Germans show to obscure university professors the deference accorded by Americans only to celebrity; the Soviets honor the holding of political power; in France a rich man is a rich man, to whom everybody grants the substantial powers that his riches command but to whom nobody grants the respect due to a member of the National Academy. But in the United States, a rich man is perceived as being necessarily both good and wise, which is an absurdity that would be seen as such not only by a Frenchman or a Russian but also by Henry James. Not that the Americans are greedier than the French, or less intellectual than the Germans, or more venal than the Russians, but to what other tribunal can an anxious and supposedly egalitarian people submit their definitions of the good, the true and the beautiful if not to the judgment of the bottom line? It is a question that James, like jesting Pilate, doesn't stay to answer. The American assumption that money rules the world is as fundamental among its titular enemies as among its nominal friends. The moralists who rage against the evils of Mammon—blaming the world's stupidity and despair on "the rich," "the banks," "the monopolists," "the robber barons," "the nabobs," "the cross of gold"—bear witness to their faith by the fervor of their blasphemy. Whether expressed as censure or praise, no other labor of the American imagination embraces so many talents and behaviors, not a few of them psychotic, as the worship of money. The offerings placed on the altars of wealth display such a bewildering infinity of forms that a true and diligent expounder of the faith would need to account not only for the price of a matched set of cruise missiles and the cost of staging Superbowl XXVIII but also for Henry David Thoreau's principled poverty, William K. Vanderbilt's stable of race horses, the diamond in the ear of the last Gould and Henry James's portrait of the city of New York.

—*Lewis* H. *Lapham,*
January 1994

25

New York Revisited

୧୬

Part One

THE SINGLE IMPRESSION or particular vision most answering to the greatness of the subject would have been, I think, a certain hour of large circumnavigation that I found prescribed, in the fulness of the spring, as the almost immediate crown of a return from the far West. I had arrived at one of the transpontine stations of the Pennsylvania Railroad; the question was of proceeding to Boston, for the occasion, without pushing through the terrible town—why "terrible," to my sense, in many ways, I shall presently explain—and the easy and agreeable attainment of this great advantage was to embark on one of the mightiest (as appeared to me) of train-bearing barges and, descending the western waters, pass round the bottom of the city and remount the other current to

Harlem; all without "losing touch" of the Pullman that had brought me from Washington. This absence of the need of losing touch, this breadth of effect, as to the whole process, involved in the prompt floating of the huge concatenated cars not only without arrest or confusion, but as for positive prodigal beguilement of the artless traveller, had doubtless much to say to the ensuing state of mind, the happily excited and amused view of the great face of New York. The extent, the ease, the energy, the quantity and number, all notes scattered about as if, in the whole business and in the splendid light, nature and science were joyously romping together, might have been taking on again, for their symbol, some collective presence of great circling and plunging, hovering and perching seabirds, white-winged images of the spirit, of the restless freedom of the Bay. The Bay had always, on other opportunities, seemed to blow its immense character straight into one's face—coming "at" you, so to speak, bearing down on you, with the full force of a thousand prows of steamers seen exactly on the line of their longitudinal axis; but I had never before been so conscious of its boundless cool assurance or seemed to see its genius so grandly at play. This was presumably indeed because I had never before enjoyed the remarkable adventure of taking in so much of the vast bristling promontory from the water, of ascending the East

River, in especial, to its upper diminishing expanses.

Something of the air of the occasion and of the mood of the moment caused the whole picture to speak with its largest suggestion; which suggestion is irresistible when once it is sounded clear. It is all, absolutely, an expression of things lately and currently *done*, done on a large impersonal stage and on the basis of inordinate gain—it is not an expression of any other matters whatever; and yet the sense of the scene (which had at several previous junctures, as well, put forth to my imagination its power), was commanding and thrilling, was in certain lights almost charming. So it befell, exactly, that an element of mystery and wonder entered into the impression—the interest of trying to make out, in the absence of features of the sort usually supposed indispensable, the reason of the beauty and the joy. It is indubitably a "great" bay, a great harbor, but no one item of the romantic, or even of the picturesque, as commonly understood, contributes to its effect.

View of New York from the south.

The shores are low and for the most part depressingly furnished and prosaically peopled; the islands, though numerous, have not a grace to exhibit, and one thinks of the other, the real flowers of geography in this order, of Naples, of Capetown, of Sydney, of Seattle, of San Francisco, of Rio, asking how if *they* justify a reputation, New York should seem to justify one. Then, after all, we remember that there are reputations and reputations; we remember above all that the imaginative response to the conditions here presented may just happen to proceed from the intellectual extravagance of the given observer. When this personage is open to corruption by almost any large view of an intensity of life, his vibrations tend to become a matter difficult even for *him* to explain. He may have to confess that the group of evident facts fails to account by itself for the complacency of his appreciation. Therefore it is that I find myself rather backward with a perceived sanction, of an at all proportionate kind, for the fine exhilaration with which, in this free wayfaring relation to them, the wide waters of New York inspire me. There is the beauty of light and air, the great scale of space, and, seen far away to the west, the open gates of the Hudson, majestic in their degree, even at a distance, and announcing still nobler things. But the real appeal, unmistakably, is in that note of vehemence in the local life of which I have spoken, for it is the appeal of a particular type of dauntless power.

The aspect the power wears then is indescribable; it is the power of the most extravagant of cities, rejoicing, as with the voice of the morning, in its might, its fortune, its unsurpassable conditions, and imparting to every object and element, to the motion and expression of every floating, hurrying, panting thing, to the throb of ferries and tugs, to the plash of waves and the play of winds and the glint of lights and the shrill of whistles and the quality and authority of breeze-borne cries—all, practically, a diffused, wasted clamor of *detonations*—something of its sharp free accent and, above all, of its sovereign sense of being "backed" and able to back. The universal *applied* passion struck me as shining unprecedentedly out of the composition; in the bigness and bravery and insolence, especially, of everything that rushed and shrieked, in the air as of a great intricate frenzied dance, half merry, half desperate, or at least half defiant, performed on the huge watery floor. This appearance of the bold lacing-together, across the waters, of the scattered members of the monstrous organism—lacing as by the ceaseless play of an enormous system of steam-shuttles or electric bobbins (I scarce know what to call them), commensurate in form with their infinite work—does perhaps more than anything else to give the pitch of the vision of energy. One has the sense that the monster grows and grows, flinging abroad its loose limbs even as some unmannered young giant at his "larks," and that the binding stitches must forever fly further and faster and draw harder; the future complexity of the web, all under the sky and over the sea, becoming thus that of some colossal set of clockworks, some steel-souled machine-room of brandished arms and hammering fists and opening and closing jaws. The immeasurable bridges are but as the horizontal sheaths of pistons working at high pressure, day and night, and subject, one apprehends with perhaps inconsistent gloom, to certain, to fantastic, to merciless multiplication. In the light of this apprehension indeed the breezy brightness of the Bay puts on the semblance of the vast white page that awaits beyond any other perhaps the black overscoring of science.

The three Brooklyn bridges.

Let me hasten to add that its present whiteness is precisely its charming note, the frankest of the signs you recognize and remember it by. That is the distinction I was
just feeling my way to name as the main ground of its
doing so well, for effect, without technical scenery. There
are great imposing ports—Glasgow and Liverpool and
London—that have already their page blackened almost
beyond redemption from any such light of the picturesque
as can hope to irradiate fog and grime, and there are others, Marseilles and Constantinople say, or, for all I know
to the contrary, New Orleans, that contrive to abound
before everything else in color, and so to make a rich and
instant and obvious show. But memory, and the actual
impression, keep investing New York with the tone, predominantly, of summer dawns and winter frosts, of sea-
foam, of bleached sails and stretched awnings, of blanched
hulls, of scoured decks, of new ropes, of polished brasses,
of streamers clear in the blue air; and it is by this harmony, doubtless, that the projection of the individual character of the place, of the candor of its avidity and the fresh-
ness of its audacity, is most conveyed. The "tall buildings,"
which have so promptly usurped a glory that affects you
as rather surprised, as yet, at itself, the multitudinous sky-
scrapers standing up to the view, from the water, like
extravagant pins in a cushion already overplanted, and
stuck in as in the dark, anywhere and anyhow, have at

least the felicity of carrying out the fairness of tone, of taking the sun and the shade in the manner of towers of marble. They are not all of marble, I believe, by any means,
even if some may be, but they are impudently new and
still more impudently "novel"—this in common with so
many other terrible things in America—and they are triumphant payers of dividends; all of which uncontested and
unabashed pride, with flash of innumerable windows and
flicker of subordinate gilt attributions, is like the flare, up
and down their long, narrow faces, of the lamps of some
general permanent "celebration."

You see the pincushion in profile, so to speak, on passing between Jersey City and Twenty-third Street, but you
get it broadside on, this loose nosegay of architectural
flowers, if you skirt the Battery, well out, and embrace the
whole plantation. Then the "American beauty," the rose of
interminable stem, becomes the token of the cluster at
large—to that degree that, positively, this is all that is
wanted for emphasis of your final impression. Such
growths, you feel, have confessedly arisen but to be
"picked," in time, with a shears; nipped short off, by waiting fate, as soon as "science," applied to gain, has put
upon the table, from far up its sleeve, some more winning
card. Crowned not only with no history, but with no cred-
ible possibility of time for history, and consecrated by no
uses save the commercial at any cost, they are simply the

most piercing notes in that concert of the expensively provisional into which your supreme sense of New York
resolves itself. They never begin to speak to you, in the
manner of the builded majesties of the world as we have
heretofore known such—towers or temples or fortresses or
palaces—with the authority of things of permanence or
even of things of long duration. One story is good only till
another is told, and sky-scrapers are the last word of economic ingenuity only till another word be written. This
shall be possibly a word of still uglier meaning, but the
vocabulary of thrift at any price shows boundless
resources, and the consciousness of that truth, the consciousness of the finite, the menaced, the essentially *invented*
state, twinkles ever, to my perception, in the thousand

The skyline of 1908.

glassy eyes of these giants of the mere market. Such a structure as the comparatively windowless bell-tower of Giotto, in Florence, looks supremely serene in its beauty. You don't feel it to have risen by the breath of an interested passion that, restless beyond all passions, is forever seeking more pliable forms. Beauty has been the object of its creator's idea, and, having found beauty, it has found the form in which it splendidly rests.

Beauty indeed was the aim of the creator of the spire of Trinity Church, so cruelly overtopped and so barely distinguishable, from your train-bearing barge, as you stand off, in its abject helpless humility; and it may of course be asked how much of this superstition finds voice in the actual shrunken presence of that laudable effort. Where, for the eye, is the felicity of simplified Gothic, of noble preeminence, that once made of this highly pleasing edifice the pride of the town and the feature of Broadway? The answer is, as obviously, that these charming elements are still there, just where they ever were, but that they have been mercilessly deprived of their visibility. It aches and throbs, this smothered visibility, we easily feel, in its caged and dishonored condition, supported only by the consciousness that the dishonor is no fault of its own. We commune with it, in tenderness and pity, through the encumbered air; our eyes, made, however unwillingly, at home in strange vertiginous upper atmospheres, look down

Trinity Church.

on it as on a poor ineffectual thing, an architectural object addressed, even in its prime aspiration, to the patient pedestrian sense and permitting thereby a relation of intimacy. It was to speak to me audibly enough on two or three other occasions—even through the thick of that frenzy of Broadway just where Broadway receives from Wall Street the fiercest application of the maddening lash; it was to put its tragic case there with irresistible lucidity. "Yes, the wretched figure I am making is as little as you see my fault—it is the fault of the buildings whose very first care is to deprive churches of their visibility. There are but two or three—two or three outward and visible churches—left in New York 'anyway,' as you must have noticed, and even they are hideously threatened: a fact at which no one, indeed, appears to be shocked, from which no one draws the least of the inferences that stick straight out of it, which every one seems in short to take for granted either with remarkable stupidity or with remarkable cynicism." So, at any rate, they may still effectively communicate, ruddy-brown (where not browny-black) old Trinity and any pausing, any attending survivor of the clearer age— and there is yet more of the bitterness of history to be tasted in such a tacit passage, as I shall presently show.

Was it not the bitterness of history, meanwhile, that on that day of circumnavigation, that day of highest intensity of impression, of which I began by speaking, the ancient rotunda of Castle Garden, viewed from just opposite, should have lurked there as a vague nonentity? One had known it from far, far back and with the indelibility of the childish vision—from the time when it was the commodious concert-hall of New York, the firmament of long-extinguished stars; in spite of which extinction there out-lives for me the image of the infant phenomenon Adelina Patti, whom (another large-eyed infant) I had been benevolently taken to hear: Adelina Patti, in a fanlike little white frock and "pantalettes" and a hussarlike red jacket, mounted on an armchair, its back supporting her, wheeled to the front of the stage and warbling like a tiny thrush even in the nest. Shabby, shrunken, barely discernible to-day, the ancient rotunda, adjusted to other uses, had afterwards, for many decades, carried on a conspicuous life—and it was the present remoteness, the repudiated barbarism of all this, foreshortened by one's own experience, that dropped the acid into the cup. The sky-scrapers and the league-long bridges, present and to come, marked the point where the age—the age for which Castle Garden could have been, in its day, a "value"—had come out. That in itself was nothing—ages do come out, as a matter of course, so far from where they have gone in. But it had done so, the latter half of the nineteenth century, in one's own more or less immediate presence; the difference, from pole to pole, was so vivid and concrete that no single shade of any one of its aspects was lost. This impact of the whole condensed past at once produced a horrible, hateful sense of personal antiquity.

Yet was it after all that those monsters of the mere market as I have called them, had more to say, on the question of "effect," than I had at first allowed?—since they are the element that looms largest for me through a particular impression, with remembered parts and pieces melting together rather richly now, of "down-town" seen and felt from the inside. "Felt"—I use that word, I dare say, all presumptuously, for a relation to matters of magnitude and mystery that I could begin neither to measure nor to penetrate, hovering about them only in magnanimous wonder, staring at them as at a world of immovably closed doors behind which immense "material" lurked, material for the artist, the painter of life, as we say, who shouldn't have begun so early and so fatally to fall away from possible initiations. This sense of a baffled curiosity, an intellectual adventure forever renounced, was surely enough a state of feeling, and indeed in presence of the different half-hours, as memory presents them, at which I gave myself up both to the thrill of Wall Street (by which I mean that of the whole wide edge of the whirlpool), and the too accepted, too irredeemable ignorance, I am at a loss to see what intensity of response was wanting. The imagination might have responded more if there had been a slightly less settled inability to understand what every one, what any one, was really doing; but the picture, as it comes back to me, is, for all this foolish subjective poverty, so crowded with its features that I rejoice, I confess, in not having more of them to handle. No open apprehension, even if it be as open as a public vehicle plying for hire, can carry more than a certain amount of life, of a kind; and there was nothing at play in the outer air, at least, of the scene, during these glimpses, that didn't scramble for admission into mine very much as I had seen the mob seeking entrance to an up-town or a down-town electric car fight for life at one of the apertures. If it had been the final function of the Bay to make one feel one's age, so, assuredly, the mouth of Wall Street proclaimed it, for one's private ear, distinctly enough; the breath of existence being taken, wherever one turned, as that of youth on the run and with the prize of the race in sight, and the new landmarks crushing the old quite as violent children stamp on snails and caterpillars.

The hour I first recall was a morning of winter drizzle and mist, of dense fog in the Bay, one of the strangest sights of which I was on my way to enjoy; and I had stopped in the heart of the business quarter to pick up a friend who was to be my companion. The weather, such as it was, worked wonders for the upper reaches of the buildings, round which it drifted and hung very much as about the flanks and summits of emergent mountain-masses—for, to be just all round, there *was* some evidence of their having a message for the eyes. Let me parenthesize, once for all, that there are other glimpses of this message, up and down the city, frequently to be caught; lights and shades of winter and summer air, of the literally "finishing" afternoon in particular, when refinement of modelling descends from the skies and lends the white towers, all new and crude and commercial and over-windowed as they are, a fleeting distinction. The morning I speak of offered me my first chance of seeing one of them from the inside—which was an opportunity I sought again, repeatedly, in respect to others; and I became conscious of the force with which this vision of their prodigious working, and of the multitudinous life, as if each were a swarming city in itself, that they are capable of housing, may beget, on the part of the free observer, in other words of the restless analyst, the impulse to describe and present the facts and express the sense of them. Each of these huge constructed and compressed communities, throbbing, through its myriad arteries and pores, with a single passion, even as a complicated watch throbs with the one purpose of telling you the hour and the minute, testified overwhelmingly to the *character* of New York—and the passion of the restless analyst, on his side, is for the extraction of character. But there would be too much to say, just here, were this incurable eccentric to let himself go; the impression in question, fed by however brief an experience, kept overflowing the cup and spreading in a wide waste of speculation. I must dip into these depths, if it prove possible, later on; let me content myself, for the moment, with remembering how from the first, on all such ground, my thought went straight to poor great wonder-working Émile Zola and *his* love of the human aggregation, the artificial microcosm, which had to spend itself on great shops, great businesses, great "apartment-houses," of inferior, of mere Parisian scale. His image, it seemed to me, really asked for compassion—in the presence of this material that his energy of evocation, his alone, would have been of a stature to meddle with. What if *Le Ventre de Paris*, what if *Au Bonheur des Dames*, what if *Pot-Bouille* and *L'Argent*, could but have come into being under the New York inspiration?

The answer to that, however, for the hour, was that, in all probability, New York was not going (as it turns such remarks) to produce both the maximum of "business" spectacle and the maximum of ironic reflection of it. Zola's huge reflector got itself formed, after all, in a far other air; it had hung there, in essence, awaiting the scene that was to play over it, long before the scene really approached it in scale. The reflecting surfaces, of the ironic, of the epic order, suspended in the New York atmosphere, have yet to show symptoms of shining out, and the monstrous phe-

43

nomena themselves, meanwhile, strike me as having, with
their immense momentum, got the start, got ahead of, in
proper parlance, any possibility of poetic, of dramatic capture. That conviction came to me most perhaps while I
gazed across at the special sky-scraper that overhangs poor
old Trinity to the north—a south face as high and wide as
the mountain-wall that drops the Alpine avalanche, from
time to time, upon the village, and the village spire, at its
foot; the interest of this case being above all, as I learned,
to my stupefaction, in the fact that the very creators of the
extinguisher are the churchwardens themselves, or at least
the trustees of the church property. What was the case but
magnificent for pitiless ferocity?—that inexorable law of
the growing invisibility of churches, their everywhere
reduced or abolished *presence*, which is nine-tenths of their
virtue, receiving thus, at such hands, its supreme consecration. This consecration was positively the greater that just
then, as I have said, the vast money-making structure quite
horribly, quite romantically justified itself, looming through
the weather with an insolent clifflike sublimity. The weather, for all that experience, mixes intimately with the fulness
of my impression; speaking not least, for instance, of the
way "the state of the streets" and the assault of the turbid
air seemed all one with the look, the tramp, the whole
quality and *allure*, the consummate monotonous common-
ness, of the pushing male crowd, moving in its dense

mass—with the confusion carried to chaos for any intelligence, any perception; a welter of objects and sounds in which relief, detachment, dignity, meaning perished utterly and lost all rights. It appeared, the muddy medium, all one with every other element and note as well, all the signs of the heaped industrial battle-field, all the sounds and silences, grim, pushing, trudging silences too, of the universal will to move—to move, move, move, as an end in itself, an appetite at any price.

In the Bay, the rest of the morning, the dense raw fog that delayed the big boat, allowing sight but of the immediate ice-masses through which it thumped its way, was not less of the essence. Anything blander, as a medium, would have seemed a mockery of the facts of the terrible little Ellis Island, the first harbor of refuge and stage of patience for the million or so of immigrants annually knocking at our official door. Before this door, which opens to them there only with a hundred forms and ceremonies, grindings and grumblings of the key, they stand appealing and waiting, marshalled, herded, divided, subdivided, sorted, sifted, searched, fumigated, for longer or shorter periods—the effect of all which prodigious process, an intendedly "scientific" feeding of the mill, is again to give the earnest observer a thousand more things to think of than he can pretend to retail. The impression of Ellis Island, in fine, would be—as I was to find throughout that so many of my impressions would be—a chapter by itself; and with a particular page for recognition of the degree in which the liberal hospitality of the eminent Commissioner of this wonderful service, to whom I had been introduced, helped to make the interest of the whole watched drama poignant and unforgettable. It is a drama that goes on, without a pause, day by day and year by year, this visible act of ingurgitation on the part of our body politic and social, and constituting really an appeal to amazement beyond that of any sword-swallowing or fire-swallowing of the circus. The wonder that one couldn't keep down was the thought that these two or three hours of one's own chance vision of the business were but as a tick or two of the mighty clock, the clock that never, never stops—least of all when it strikes, for a sign of so much winding-up, some louder hour of our national fate than usual. I think indeed that the simplest account of the action of Ellis Island on the spirit of any sensitive citizen who may have happened to "look in" is that he comes back from his visit not at all the same person that he went. He has eaten of the tree of knowledge, and the taste will be forever in his mouth. He had thought he knew before, thought he had the sense of the degree in which it is his American fate to share the sanctity of his American consciousness, the intimacy of his American patriotism, with the inconceivable alien; but the truth had never come home to him with any such force. In the lurid light projected upon it by those courts of dismay, it shakes him—or I like at least to imagine it shakes him—to the depths of his being; I like to think of him, I positively *have* to think of him, as going about ever afterwards with a new look, for those who can see it, in his face, the outward sign of the new chill in his heart. So is stamped, for detection, the questionably privileged person who has had an apparition, seen a ghost in his supposedly safe old house. Let not the unwary, therefore, visit Ellis Island.

The after-sense of that acute experience, however, I myself found, was by no means to be brushed away; I felt it grow and grow, on the contrary, wherever I turned: other impressions might come and go, but this affirmed claim of the alien, however immeasurably alien, to share in one's supreme relation was everywhere the fixed element, the reminder not to be dodged. One's supreme relation, as one had always put it, was one's relation to one's country—a conception made up so largely of one's countrymen and one's countrywomen. Thus it was as if, all the while, with such a fond tradition of what these products predominantly were, the idea of the country itself underwent something of that profane overhauling through which it appears to suffer the indignity of change. Is not our instinct in this matter, in general, essentially the safe one— that of keeping the idea simple and strong and continuous, so that it shall be perfectly sound? To touch it overmuch, to pull it about, is to put it in peril of weakening; yet on this free assault upon it, this readjustment of it in *their* monstrous, presumptuous interest, the aliens, in New York, seemed perpetually to insist. The combination there of their quantity and their quality—that loud primary stage of alienism which New York most offers to sight—operates, for the native, as their note of settled possession, something they have nobody to thank for; so that *un*settled possession is what we, on our side, seem reduced to—the implication of which, in its turn, is that, to recover confidence and regain lost ground, we, not they, must make the surrender and accept the orientation. We must go, in other words, *more* than half-way to meet them; which is all the difference, for us, between possession and dispossession. This sense of dispossession, to be brief about it, haunted me so, I was to feel, in the New York streets and in the packed trajectiles to which one clingingly appeals from the streets, just as one tumbles back into the streets in appalled reaction from *them*, that the art of beguiling or duping it became an art to be cultivated—though the fond alternative vision was never long to be obscured, the imagination, exasperated to envy, of the ideal, in the order in question; of the luxury of some such close and sweet and *whole* national consciousness as that of the Switzer and the Scot.

Part Two

৯৯

MY RECOVERY OF IMPRESSIONS, after a short interval, yet with their flush a little faded, may have been judged to involve itself with excursions of memory—memory directed to the antecedent time—reckless almost to extravagance. But I recall them to-day, none the less, for that value in them which ministered, at happy moments, to an artful evasion of the actual. There was no escape from the ubiquitous alien into the future, or even into the present; there was an escape but into the past. I count as quite a triumph in this interest an unbroken ease of frequentation of that ancient end of Fifth Avenue to the whole neighborhood of which one's earlier vibrations, a very far-away matter now, were attuned. The precious stretch of space between Washington Square and Fourteenth Street had a value, had even a charm, for the revisiting spirit—a mild and melancholy glamour which I am conscious of the difficulty of "rendering" for new and heedless generations.

Here again the assault of suggestion is too great; too large, I mean, the number of hares started, before the pursuing imagination, the quickened memory, by this fact of the felt moral and social value of this comparatively unimpaired morsel of the Fifth Avenue heritage. Its reference to a pleasanter, easier, hazier past is absolutely comparative, just as the past in question itself enjoys as such the merest courtesy-title. It is all recent history enough, by the measure of the whole, and there are flaws and defacements enough, surely, even in its appearance of decency of duration. The tall building, grossly tall and grossly ugly, has failed of an admirable chance of distinguished consideration for it, and the dignity of many of its peaceful fronts has succumbed to the presence of those industries whose foremost need is to make "a good thing" of them. The good thing is doubtless being made, and yet this lower end of the once agreeable street still just escapes being a wholly bad thing. What held the fancy in thrall, however, as I say, was the admonition, proceeding from all the facts, that values of this romantic order are at best, anywhere, strangely relative. It was an extraordinary statement on the subject of New York that the space between Fourteenth Street and Washington Square *should* count for "tone," figure as the old ivory of an overscored tablet.

True wisdom, I found, was to let it, to make it, so count and figure as much as it would, and charming assistance

came for this, I also found, from the young good-nature of
May and June. There had been neither assistance nor
good-nature during the grim weeks of mid-winter; there
had been but the meagre fact of a discomfort and an ugliness less formidable here than elsewhere. When, toward
the top of the town, circulation, alimentation, recreation,
every art of existence, gave way before the full onset of
winter, when the upper avenues had become as so many
congested bottle-necks, through which the wine of life simply refused to be decanted, getting back to these latitudes
resembled really a return from the North Pole to the
Temperate Zone: it was as if the wine of life had been
poured for you, in advance, into some pleasant old punch-
bowl that would support you through the temporary stress.
Your condition was not reduced to the endless vista of a
clogged tube, of a thoroughfare occupied as to the narrow
central ridge with trolley-cars stuffed to suffocation, and as
to the mere margin, on either side, with snow-banks result-
ing from the cleared rails and offering themselves as a field
for all remaining action. Free existence and good manners,
in New York, are too much brought down to a bare rigor
of marginal relation to the endless electric coil, the monstrous chain that winds round the general neck and body,
the general middle and legs, very much as the boa-con-
strictor winds round the group of the Laocoon. It struck
me that when these folds are tightened in the terrible stric-

ture of the snow-smothered months of the year, the New
York predicament leaves far behind the anguish represent-
ed in the Vatican figures. To come and go where East
Eleventh Street, where West Tenth, opened their kind
short arms was at least to keep clear of the awful hug of
the serpent. And this was a grace that grew large, as I
have hinted, with the approach of summer and that made
in the afternoons of May and of the first half of June,
above all, an insidious appeal. There, I repeat, was the delicacy, there the mystery, there the wonder, in especial, of
the unquenchable intensity of the impressions received in
childhood. They are made then once for all, be their intrin-
sic beauty, interest, importance, small or great; the stamp is
indelible and never wholly fades. This in fact gives it an
importance, when a lifetime has intervened. I found myself
intimately recognizing every house my officious tenth year
had, in the way of imagined adventure, introduced to me—
incomparable master of ceremonies after all; the privilege
had been offered, since, to millions of other objects that
had made nothing of it, that had gone as they came; so
that here were Fifth Avenue corners with which one's connection was fairly exquisite. The lowered light of the days'
ends of early summer became them, moreover, exceedingly,
and they fell, for the quiet northward perspective, into a
dozen delicacies of composition and tone.

One could talk of "quietness" now, for the shrinkage of

life so marked, in the higher latitudes of the town, after Easter, the visible early flight of that "society" which, by the old custom, used never to budge before June or July, had almost the effect of clearing some of the streets, and indeed of suggesting that a truly clear New York might have an unsuspected charm or two to put forth. An approach to peace and harmony might have been, in a manner, promised, and the sense of other days took advantage of it to steal abroad with a ghostly tread. It kept meeting, half the time, to its discomfiture, the lamentable little Arch of Triumph which bestrides these beginnings of

Northside of Washington Square Park.

Washington Square—lamentable because of its poor and lonely and unsupported and unaffiliated state. With this melancholy monument it could make no terms at all, but turned its back to the strange sight as often as possible, helping itself thereby, moreover, to do a little of the pretending required, no doubt, by the fond theory that nothing hereabouts was changed. Nothing *was*, it could occasionally appear to me—there was no new note in the picture, not one, for instance, when I paused before a low house in a small row on the south side of Waverley Place and lived again into the queer medieval costume (preserved by the daguerreotypist's art) of the very little boy for whom the scene had once embodied the pangs and pleasures of a Dame's small school. The Dame must have been Irish, by her name, and the Irish tradition, only intensified and coarsened, seemed still to possess the place, the fact of the survival, the sturdy sameness, of which arrested me, again and again, to fascination. The shabby red house, with its mere two stories, its lowly "stoop," its dislocated ironwork of the forties, the early fifties, the record, in its face, of blistering summers and of the long stages of the loss of self-respect, made it as consummate a morsel of the old liquor-scented, heated-looking city, the city of no pavements, but of such a plenty of politics, as I could have desired. And neighboring Sixth Avenue, overstraddled though it might be with feats of engineering unknown to the primitive age that otherwise so persisted, wanted only, to carry off the illusion, the warm smell of the bakery on the corner of Eighth Street, a blessed repository of doughnuts, cookies, creamcakes and pies, the slow passing by which, on returns from school, must have had much in common with the experience of the shipmen of old who came, in long voyages, while they tacked and hung back, upon those belts of ocean that are haunted with the balm and spice of tropic islands.

These were the felicities of the backward reach, which, however, had also its melancholy checks and snubs; nowhere quite so sharp as in presence, so to speak, of the rudely, the ruthlessly suppressed birth-house on the other side of the Square. That was where the pretence that nearly nothing was changed had most to come in; for a high, square impersonal structure, proclaiming its lack of interest with a crudity all its own, so blocks, at the right moment for its own success, the view of the past, that the effect for me, in Washington Place, was of having been amputated of half my history. The gray and more or less "hallowed" University building—wasn't it somehow, with a desperate bravery, both castellated and gabled?—has vanished from the earth, and vanished with it the two or three adjacent houses, of which the birthplace was one. This was the snub, for the complacency of retrospect, that, whereas the inner sense had positively erected there for its private con-

templation a commemorative mural tablet, the very wall
that should have borne this inscription had been smashed
as for demonstration that tablets, in New York, are
unthinkable. And I have had indeed to permit myself this
free fantasy of the hypothetic rescued identity of a given
house—taking the vanished number in Washington Place
as most pertinent—in order to invite the reader to gasp
properly with me before the fact that we not only fail to
remember, in the whole length of the city, one of these
frontal records of birth, sojourn or death, under a cele-
brated name, but that we have only to reflect an instant to
see any such form of civic piety inevitably and forever
absent. The form is cultivated, to the greatly quickened
interest of street-scenery, in many of the cities of Europe;
and is it not verily bitter, for those who feel a poetry in
the noted passage, longer or shorter, here and there, of
great lost spirits, that the institution, the profit, the glory
of any such association is denied in advance to communities tending, as the phrase is, to "run" preponderantly to
the sky-scraper? Where, in fact, is the point of inserting a
mural tablet, at any legible height, in a building certain to
be destroyed to make room for a sky-scraper? And from
where, on the other hand, in a façade of fifty floors, does
one "see" the pious plate recording the honor attached to
one of the apartments look down on a responsive people?
We have but to ask the question to recognize our neces-

sary failure to answer it as a supremely characteristic local note—a note in the light of which the great city is projected into its future as, practically, a huge continuous fifty-floored conspiracy against the very idea of the ancient graces, those that strike us as having flourished just in proportion as the parts of life and the signs of character have *not* been lumped together, not been indistinguishably sunk in the common fund of mere economic convenience. So interesting, as object-lessons, may the developments of the American gregarious ideal become; so traceable, at every turn, to the restless analyst at least, are the heavy foot-prints, in the finer texture of life, of a great commercial democracy seeking to abound supremely in its own sense and having none to gainsay it.

Let me not, however, forget, amid such contemplations, what may serve here as a much more relevant instance of the operation of values, the price of the as yet undiminished dignity of the two most southward of the Fifth Avenue churches. Half the charm of the prospect, at that extremity, is in their still being there, and being as they are; this charm, this serenity of escape and survival positively works as a blind on the side of the question of their architectural importance. The last shade of pedantry or priggishness drops from your view of that element; they illustrate again supremely your grasped truth of the *comparative* character, in such conditions, of beauty and of interest. The special standard they may or may not square with signifies, you feel, not a jot: all you know, and want to know, is that they are probably menaced—some horrible voice of the air has murmured it—and that with them will go, if fate overtakes them, the last cases worth mentioning (with a single exception,) of the modest felicity that sometimes used to be. Remarkable certainly the state of things in which mere exemption from the "squashed" condition can shed such a glamour; but we may accept the state of things if only we can keep the glamour undispelled. It reached its maximum for me, I hasten to add, on my penetrating into the Ascension, at chosen noon, and standing for the first time in presence of that noble work of John La Farge, the representation, on the west wall, in the grand manner, of the theological event from which the church takes its title. Wonderful enough, in New York, to find oneself, in a charming and considerably dim "old" church, hushed to admiration before a great religious picture; the sensation, for the moment, upset so all the facts. The hot light, outside, might have been that of an Italian *piazzetta;* the cool shade, within, with the important work of art shining through it, seemed part of some other-world pilgrimage—all the more that the important work of art itself, a thing of the highest distinction, spoke, as soon as one had taken it in, with that authority which makes the difference, ever afterwards, between the remembered and the forgotten quest. A rich note of interference came, I admit, through the splendid window-glass, the finest of which, unsurpassably fine, to my sense, is the work of the same artist; so that the church, as it stands, is very nearly as commemorative a monument as a great reputation need wish. The deeply pictorial windows, in which clearness of picture and fulness of expression consort so successfully with a tone as of magnified gems, did not strike one as looking into a yellow little square of the south—they put forth a different implication; but the flaw in the harmony was, more than anything else, that sinister voice of the air of which I have spoken, the fact that one *could* stand there, vibrating to such impressions, only to remember the suspended danger, the possibility of the doom. Here was the loveliest cluster of images, begotten on the spot, that the preoccupied city had ever taken thought to offer itself; and here, to match them, like some black shadow they had been condemned to cast, was this particular prepared honor of "removal" that appeared to hover about them.

One's fear, I repeat, was perhaps misplaced—but what an air to live in, the shuddering pilgrim mused, the air in which such fears are not misplaced only when we are conscious of very special reassurances! The vision of the doom that does descend, that had descended all round, was at all events, for the half-hour, all that was wanted to charge with the last tenderness one's memory of the transfigured

interior. Afterwards, outside, again and again, the powers
of removal struck me as looming, awfully, in the newest
mass of multiplied floors and windows visible at this point.
They, ranged in this terrible recent erection, were going to
bring in money—and was not money the only thing a self-
respecting structure could be thought of as bringing in?
Hadn't one heard, just before, in Boston, that the security,
that the sweet serenity of the Park Street Church,
charmingest, there, of aboriginal notes, the very light, with
its perfect position and its dear old delightful Wren-like
spire, of the starved city's eyes, had been artfully practised
against, and that the question of saving it might become, in
the near future, acute? Nothing, fortunately, I think, is so
much the "making" of New York, at its central point, for
the visual, almost for the romantic, sense, as the Park
Street Church is the making, by its happy coming-in, of
Boston; and, therefore, if it were thinkable that the pecu-
liar rectitude of Boston might be laid in the dust, what
mightn't easily come about for the reputedly less austere
conscience of New York? Once such questions had
obtained lodgment, to take one's walks was verily to look
at almost everything in their light; and to commune with
the sky-scraper under this influence was really to feel
worsted, more and more, in any magnanimous attempt to
adopt the æsthetic view of it. I may appear to make too
much of these invidious presences, but it must be remem-

bered that they represent, for our time, the only claim to any consideration other than merely statistical established by the resounding growth of New York. The attempt to take the æsthetic view is invariably blighted sooner or later by their most salient characteristic, *the* feature that speaks loudest for the economic idea. Window upon window, at any cost, is a condition never to be reconciled with any grace of building, and the logic of the matter here happens to put on a particularly fatal front. If quiet interspaces, always half the architectural battle, exist no more in such a structural scheme than quiet tones, blest breathing-spaces, occur, for the most part, in New York conversation, so the reason is, demonstrably, that the building can't afford them. (It is by very much the same law, one supposes, that New York conversation cannot afford stops.) The building can only afford lights, each light having a superlative value as an aid to the transaction of business and the conclusion of sharp bargains. Doesn't it take in fact acres of window-glass to help even an expert New-Yorker to get the better of another expert one, or to see that the other expert one doesn't get the better of *him*? It is easy to conceive that, after all, with this origin and nature stamped upon their foreheads, the last word of the mercenary monsters should not be their address to our sense of formal beauty.

Still, as I have already hinted, there was always the case

of the one other rescued identity and preserved felicity, the
happy accident of the elder day still ungrudged and final-
ly legitimated. When I say ungrudged, indeed, I seem to
remember how I had heard that the divine little City Hall
had *been* grudged, at a critical moment, to within an inch
of its life; had but just escaped, in the event, the extremity of grudging. It lives on securely, by the mercy of fate —
lives on in the delicacy of its beauty, speaking volumes
again (more volumes distinctly, than are anywhere else
spoken) for the exquisite truth of the *conferred* value of
interesting objects, the value derived from the social, the
civilizing function for which they have happened to find
their opportunity. It is the opportunity that gives them
their price, and the luck of there being, round about them,
nothing greater than themselves to steal it away from
them. They strike thus, practically, the supreme note,
and — such is the mysterious play of our finer sensibility! —
one takes this note, one is glad to work it, as the phrase
goes, for all it is worth. I so work the note of the City
Hall, no doubt, in speaking of the spectacle there constituted as "divine"; but I do it precisely by reason of the
spectacle taken *with* the delightful small facts of the building: largely by reason, in other words, of the elegant, the
gallant little structure's situation and history, the way it has
played, artistically, ornamentally, its part, has held out for
the good cause, through the long years, alone and unpro-

tected. The fact is it has been the very centre of that assault of vulgarity of which the innumerable mementos rise within view of it and tower, at a certain distance, over it; and yet it has never parted with a square inch of its character, it has forced them, in a manner, to stand off. I hasten to add that in expressing thus its uncompromised state I speak of its outward, its æsthetic character only. So, at all events, it has discharged the civilizing function I just named as inherent in such cases—that of representing, to the community possessed of it, all the Style the community is likely to get, and of making itself responsible for the same.

The consistency of this effort, under difficulties, has been the story that brings tears to the eyes of the hovering kindly critic, and it is through his tears, no doubt, that such a personage reads the best passages of the tale and makes out the proportions of the object. Mine, I recognize, didn't prevent my seeing that the pale yellow marble (or whatever it may be) of the City Hall has lost, by some late excoriation, the remembered charm of its old surface, the pleasant promiscuous patina of time; but the perfect taste and finish, the reduced yet ample scale, the harmony of parts, the just proportions, the modest classic grace, the living look of the type aimed at, these things, with gayety of detail undiminished and "quaintness" of effect augmented, are all there; and I see them, as I write, in that glow of appreciation which made it necessary, of a fine June morning, that I should somehow pay the whole place my respects. The simplest, in fact the only way, was, obviously, to pass under the charming portico and brave the consequences: this impunity of such audacities being, in America, one of the last of the lessons the repatriated absentee finds himself learning. The crushed spirit he brings back from European discipline never quite rises to the height of the native argument, the brave sense that the public, the civic building is his very own, for any honest use, so that he may tread even its most expensive pavements and staircases (and very expensive, for the American citizen, these have lately become,) without a question asked. This further and further unchallenged penetration begets in the perverted person I speak of a really romantic thrill: it is like some assault of the dim seraglio, with the guards bribed, the eunuchs drugged and one's life carried in one's hand. The only drawback to such freedom is that penetralia it is so easy to penetrate fail a little of a due impressiveness, and that if stationed sentinels are bad for the temper of the freeman they are good for the "prestige" of the building.

Never, in any case, it seemed to me, had any freeman made so free with the majesty of things as I was to make on this occasion with the mysteries of the City Hall—even to the point of coming out into the presence of the Representative of the highest office with which City Halls are associated, and whose thoroughly gracious condonation of my act set the seal of success upon the whole adventure. Its dizziest intensity, in fact, sprang precisely from the unexpected view opened into the old official, the old so thick-peopled local, municipal world: upper chambers of council and state, delightfully of their nineteenth-century time, as to design and ornament, in spite of rank restoration; but replete, above all, with portraits of past worthies, past celebrities and city fathers, Mayors, Bosses, Presidents, Governors, Statesmen at large, Generals and Commodores at large, florid ghosts, looking so unsophisticated now, of years not remarkable, municipally, for the absence of

City Hall, New York, 1900.

sophistication. Here were types, running mainly to ugliness and all bristling with the taste of their day and the quite touching provincialism of their conditions, as to many of which nothing would be more interesting than a study of New York annals in the light of their personal look, their very noses and mouths and complexions and heads of hair—to say nothing of their waistcoats and neckties; with such color, such sound and movement would the thick stream of local history then be interfused. Wouldn't its thickness fairly become transparent? since to walk through the collection was not only to see and feel so much that had happened, but to understand, with the truth again and again inimitably pointed, why nothing could have happened otherwise; the whole array thus presenting itself as an unsurpassed demonstration of the real reasons of things. The florid ghosts look out from their exceedingly gilded frames—all that *that* can do is bravely done for them— with the frankest responsibility for everything; their collective presence becomes a kind of copious telltale document signed with a hundred names. There are few of these that at this hour, I think, we particularly desire to repeat; but the place where they may be read is, all the way from river to river and from the Battery to Harlem, the place in which there is most of the terrible town.

Main foyer — Waldorf-Astoria Hotel.

Concluded

৯▲

IF THE BAY HAD SEEMED TO ME, as I have noted, most to help the fond observer of New York aspects to a sense, through the eyes, of embracing possession, so the part played there for the outward view found its match for the inward in the portentous impression of one of the great caravansaries administered to me of a winter afternoon. I say with intention "administered": on so assiduous a guide, through the endless labyrinth of the Waldorf-Astoria was I happily to chance after turning out of the early dusk and the January sleet and slosh into permitted, into enlightened contemplation of a pandemonium not less admirably ordered, to all appearance, than rarely intermitted. The seer of great cities is liable to easy error, I know, when he finds this, that or the other caught glimpse the supremely significant one—and I am willing to preface with that remark my confession that New York told me more of her story at once, then and there, than she was again and else-

where to tell. With this apprehension that she was in fact
fairly shrieking it into one's ears came a curiosity, corre-
sponding, as to its kind and its degree of interest; so that
there was nought to do, as we picked our tortuous way,
but to stare with all our eyes and miss as little as possible
of the revelation. That harshness of the essential conditions, the outward, which almost any large attempt at the
amenities, in New York, has to take account of and make
the best of, has at least the effect of projecting the visitor
with force upon the spectacle prepared for him at this particular point and of marking the more its sudden high
pitch, the character of violence which all its warmth, its
color and glitter so completely muffle. There is violence
outside, mitigating sadly the frontal majesty of the monument, leaving it exposed to the vulgar assault of the street
by the operation of those dire facts of absence of margin,
of meagreness of site, of the brevity of the block, of the
inveteracy of the near thoroughfare, which leave "style," in
construction, at the mercy of the impertinent cross-streets,
make detachment and independence, save in the rarest
cases, an insoluble problem, preclude without pity any element of court or garden, and open to the builder in quest
of distinction the one alternative, and the great adventure,
of seeking his reward in the sky.

Of their license to pursue it there to any extent whatever New-Yorkers are, I think, a trifle too assertively

proud; no court of approach, no interspace worth mention, ever forming meanwhile part of the ground-plan or helping to receive the force of the breaking public wave. New York pays at this rate the penalty of her primary topographic curse, her old inconceivably bourgeois scheme of composition and distribution, the uncorrected labor of minds with no imagination of the future and blind before the opportunity given them by their two magnificent water-fronts. This original sin of the longitudinal avenues perpetually, yet meanly intersected, and of the organized sacrifice of the indicated alternative, the great perspectives from East to West, might still have earned forgiveness by some occasional departure from its pettifogging consistency. But, thanks to this consistency, the city is, of all great cities, the least endowed with any blest item of stately square or goodly garden, with any happy accident or surprise, any fortunate nook or casual corner, any deviation, in fine, into the liberal or the charming. That way, however, for the regenerate filial mind, madness may be said to lie — the way of imagining what might have been and putting it all together in the light of what so helplessly is. One of the things that helplessly are, for instance, is just this assault of the street, as I have called it, upon any direct dealing with our caravansary. The electric cars, with their double track, are everywhere almost as tight a fit in the narrow channel of the roadway as the projectile in the bore of a gun; so that the Waldorf-Astoria, sitting by this absent margin for life with her open lap and arms, is reduced to confessing, with a strained smile, across the traffic and the danger, how little, outside her mere swing-door, she can do for you. She seems to admit that the attempt to get at her may cost you your safety, but reminds you at the same time that any good American, and even any good inquiring stranger, is supposed willing to risk that boon for her. *"Un bon mouvement*, therefore: you must make a dash for it, but you'll see I'm worth it."* If such a claim as this last be ever justified, it would indubitably be justified here; the survivor scrambling out of the current and up the bank finds in the amplitude of the entertainment awaiting him an instant sense as of applied restoratives. The amazing hotel-world quickly closes round him; with the process of transition reduced to its minimum he is transported to conditions of extraordinary complexity and brilliancy, operating—and with proportionate perfection—by laws of their own and expressing after their fashion a complete scheme of life. The air swarms, to intensity, with the *characteristic,* the characteristic condensed and accumulated as he rarely elsewhere has had the luck to find it. It jumps out to meet his every glance, and this unanimity of its spring, of all its aspects and voices, is what I just now referred to as the essence of the loud New York story. That effect of violence, in the whole communication, at which I thus hint, results from the inordinate mass, the quantity of presence, as it were, of the testimony heaped together for emphasis of the wondrous moral.

The moral in question, the high interest of the tale, is that you are in presence of a revelation of the possibilities of the hotel—for which the American spirit has found so unprecedented a use and a value; leading it on to express so a social, indeed positively an æsthetic ideal, and making it so, at this supreme pitch, a synonym for civilization, for the capture of conceived manners themselves, that one is verily tempted to ask if the hotel spirit may not just *be* the American spirit most seeking and most finding itself. That truth—the truth that the present is more and more the day of the hotel—had not waited to burst on the mind at the view of this particular establishment; we have all more or less been educated to it, the world over, by the fruit-bearing action of the American example: in consequence of which it has been opened to us to see still other societies moved by the same irresistible spring and trying, with whatever grace and ease they may bring to the business, to unlearn as many as possible of their old social canons, and in especial their old discrimination in favor of the private life. The business for them—for communities to which the American ease in such matters is not native—goes much less of itself and produces as yet a scantier show; the great difference with the American show being that, in the United States, every one is, for the lubrication of the general machinery, practically in everything, whereas, in Europe, mostly, it is only certain people who are in anything; so that the machinery, so much less generalized, works in a smaller, stiffer way. This one caravansary makes the American case vivid, gives it, you feel, that quantity of illustration which renders the place a new thing under the sun. It is an expression of the gregarious state breaking down every barrier but two—one of which, the barrier consisting of the high pecuniary tax, is the immediately obvious. The other, the rather more subtle, is the condition, for any member of the flock, that he or she—in other words especially she—be presumably "respectable," be, that is, not discoverably anything else. The rigor with which any appearance of pursued or desired adventure is kept down—adventure in the florid sense of the word, the sense in which it remains an euphemism—is not the least interesting note of the whole immense promiscuity. Protected at those two points the promiscuity carries, through the rest of the range, everything before it.

It sat there, it walked and talked, and ate and drank, and listened and danced to music, and otherwise revelled and roamed, and bought and sold, and came and went there, all on its own splendid terms and with an encompassing material splendor, a wealth and variety of constituted picture and background, that might well feed it with the finest illusions about itself. It paraded through halls and saloons in which art and history, in masquerading dress, muffled almost to suffocation as in the gold brocade of their pretended majesties and their conciliatory graces, stood smirking on its passage with the last cynicism of hypocrisy. The exhibition is wonderful for that, for the suggested sense of a promiscuity which manages to be at the same time an inordinate untempered monotony; manages to be so, on such ground as this, by an extraordinary trick of its own, wherever one finds it. The combination forms I think, largely, the very interest, such as it is, of these phases of the human scene in the United States—if only for the pleasant puzzle of our wondering how, when types, aspects, conditions, have so much in common, they should seem at all to make up a conscious miscellany. That question, however, the question of the play and range, the practical elasticity, of the social sameness, in America, will meet us elsewhere on our path, and I confess that all questions gave way, in my mind, to a single irresistible obsession. This was just the ache of envy of the spirit of a society which had found there, in its prodigious public setting, so exactly what it wanted. One was in presence, as never before, of a realized ideal and of that childlike rush of surrender to it and clutch at it which one was so repeatedly to recognize, in America, as the note of the supremely gregarious state. It made the whole vision unforgettable, and

I am now carried back to it, I confess, in musing hours, as to one of my few glimpses of perfect human felicity. It had the admirable sign that it was, precisely, so comprehensively collective—that it made so vividly, in the old phrase, for the greatest happiness of the greatest number. Its rare beauty, one felt with instant clarity of perception, was that it was, for a "mixed" social manifestation, blissfully exempt from any principle or possibility of disaccord with itself. It was absolutely a fit to its conditions, those conditions which were both its earth and its heaven, and every part of the picture, every item of the immense sum, every wheel of the wondrous complexity, was on the best terms with all the rest.

The sense of these things became for the hour as the golden glow in which one's envy burned, and through which, while the sleet and the slosh, and the clangorous charge of cars, and the hustling, hustled crowds held the outer world, one carried one's charmed attention from one chamber of the temple to another. For that is how the place speaks, as great constructed and achieved harmonies mostly speak—as a temple builded, with clustering chapels and shrines, to an idea. The hundreds and hundreds of people in circulation, the innumerable huge-hatted ladies in especial, with their air of finding in the gilded and storied labyrinth the very firesides and pathways of home, became thus the serene faithful, whose rites one would no more have sceptically brushed than one would doff one's disguise in a Mohammedan mosque. The question of who they all might be, seated under palms and by fountains, or communing, to some inimitable New York tune, with the shade of Marie Antoinette in the queer recaptured actuality of an easy Versailles or an intimate Trianon—such questions as that, interesting in other societies and at other times, insisted on yielding here to the mere eloquence of the general truth. Here was a social order in positively stable equilibrium. Here was a world whose relation to its form and medium was practically imperturbable; here was a conception of publicity *as* the vital medium organized with the authority with which the American genius for organization, put on its mettle, alone could organize it. The whole thing remains for me, however, I repeat, a gorgeous golden blur, a paradise peopled with unmistakable American shapes, yet in which, the general and the particular, the organized and the extemporized, the element of ingenuous joy below and of consummate management above, melted together and left one uncertain which of them one was, at a given turn of the maze, most admiring. When I reflect indeed that without my clue I should not have even known the maze—should not have known, at the given turn, whether I was engulfed, for instance, in the *vente de charité* of the theatrical profession and the onset of persuasive peddling actresses, or in the annual tea-party of German lady-patronesses (of I know not what) filling with their Oriental opulence and their strange idiom a playhouse of the richest rococo, where some other expensive anniversary, the ball of a guild or the carouse of a club, was to tread on their heels and instantly mobilize away their paraphernalia—when I so reflect I see the sharpest dazzle of the eyes as precisely the play of the genius for organization.

There are a thousand forms of this ubiquitous American force, the most ubiquitous of all, that I was in no position to measure; but there was often no resisting a vivid view of the form it may take, on occasion, under pressure of the native conception of the hotel. Encountered embodiments of the gift, in this connection, master-spirits of management whose influence was as the very air, the very expensive air, one breathed, abide with me as the intensest examples of American character; indeed as the very interesting supreme examples of a type which has even on the American ground, doubtless, not said its last word, but which has at least treated itself there to a luxury of development. It gives the impression, when at all directly met, of having at its service something of that fine flame that makes up personal greatness; so that, again and again, as I found, one would have liked to see it more intimately at work. Such failures of opportunity and of penetration, however, are but the daily bread of the visionary tourist. Whenever I dip back, in fond memory, none the less, into the vision I have here attempted once more to call up, I see the whole thing overswept as by the colossal extended arms, waving the magical bâton, of some high-stationed orchestral leader, the absolute presiding power, conscious of every note of every instrument, controlling and commanding the whole volume of sound, keeping the whole effect together and making it what it is. What may one say of such a spirit if not that he understands, so to speak, the forces he sways, understands his boundless American material and plays with it like a master indeed? One sees it thus, in its crude plasticity, almost in the likeness of an army of puppets whose strings the wealth of his technical imagination teaches him innumerable ways of pulling, and yet whose innocent, whose always ingenuous agitation of their members he has found means to make them think of themselves as delightfully free and easy. Such was my impression of the perfection of the concert that, for fear of its being spoiled by some chance false note, I never went into the place again.

It might meanwhile seem no great adventure merely to walk the streets; but (beside the fact that there is, in general, never a better way of taking in life,) this pursuit irresistibly solicited, on the least pretext, the observer whose impressions I note—accustomed as he had ever been conscientiously to yield to it: more particularly with the relenting year, when the breath of spring, mildness being really installed, appeared the one vague and disinterested presence in the place, the one presence not vociferous and clamorous. Any definite presence that doesn't bellow and bang takes on in New York by that simple fact a distinction practically exquisite; so that one goes forth to meet it as a guest of honor, and that, for my own experience, I remember certain aimless strolls as snatches of intimate communion with the spirit of May and June—as abounding, almost to enchantment, in the comparatively *still* condition. Two secrets, at this time, seemed to profit by that influence to tremble out; one of these to the effect that New York would really have been "meant" to be charming, and the other to the effect that the restless analyst, willing at the lightest persuasion to let so much of its ugliness edge away unscathed from his analysis, must have had for it, from far back, one of those loyalties that are beyond any reason.

"It's all very well," the voice of the air seemed to say, if I may so take it up; "it's all very well to 'criticise,' but you distinctly take an interest and are the victim of your interest, be the grounds of your perversity what they will. You can't escape from it, and don't you see that that, precisely, is what *makes* an adventure for you (an adventure, I admit, as with some strident, battered, questionable beauty, truly some 'bold bad' charmer,) of almost any odd stroll, or waste half-hour, or other promiscuous passage, that results for you in an impression? There is always your bad habit of receiving through almost any accident of vision more

impressions than you know what to do with; but that, for
common convenience, is your eternal handicap and may
not be allowed to plead here against your special responsibility. You *care* for the terrible town, yea even for the 'horrible,' as I have overheard you call it, or at least think it,
when you supposed no one would know; and you see now
how, if you fly such fancies as that it was conceivably
meant to be charming, you are tangled by that weakness in
some underhand imagination of its possibly, one of these
days, as a riper fruit of time, becoming so. To do that, you
indeed sneakingly provide, it must get away from itself;
but you are ready to follow its hypothetic dance even to
the mainland and to the very end of its tether. What
makes the general relation of your adventure with it is
that, at bottom, you are all the while wondering, in presence of the aspects of its genius and its shame, what elements or parts, if any, would be worth its saving, worth
carrying off for the fresh embodiment and the better life,
and which of them would have, on the other hand, to face
the notoriety of going *first* by the board. I have literally
heard you qualify the monster as 'shameless'—though that
was wrung from you, I admit, by the worst of the winter
conditions, when circulation, in any fashion consistent with
personal decency or dignity, was merely mocked at, when
the stony-hearted 'trolleys,' cars of Juggernaut in their
power to squash, triumphed all along the line, when the

February blasts became as cyclones in the darkened gorges
of masonry (which down-town, in particular, put on, at
their mouths, the semblance of black rat-holes, holes of
gigantic rats, inhabited by whirlwinds); when all the pre-
tences and impunities and infirmities, in fine, had massed
themselves to be hurled at you in the fury of the elements,
in the character of the traffic, in the unadapted state of the
place to almost *any* dense movement, and, beyond everything, in that pitch of all the noises which acted on your
nerves as so much wanton provocation, so much conscious
cynicism. The fury of sound took the form of derision of
the rest of your woe, and thus it *might*, I admit, have
struck you as brazen that the horrible place should, in
such confessed collapse, still be swaggering and shouting.
It might have struck you that great cities, with the eyes of
the world on them, as the phrase is, should be capable
either of a proper form or (failing this) of a proper com-
punction; which tributes to propriety were, on the part of
New York, equally wanting. This made you remark, precisely, that nothing was wanting, on the other hand, to that
analogy with the character of the bad bold beauty, the
creature the most blatant of whose pretensions is that she
is one of those to whom everything is always forgiven. On
what ground 'forgiven'? of course you ask; but note that
you ask it while you're in the very act of forgiving. Oh
yes, you are; you've as much as said so yourself. So there

A city in a street — Nassau Street in Lower New York.

it all is; arrange it as you can. Poor dear bad bold beauty;
there must indeed be something about her—!"

Let me grant then, to get on, that there *was* doubtless,
in the better time, something about her; there was enough
about her, at all events, to conduce to that distinct cultiva-
tion of her company for which the contemplative stroll,
when there was time for it, was but another name. The
analogy was in truth complete; since the repetition of such
walks, and the admission of the beguiled state contained in
them, resembled nothing so much as the visits so often still
incorrigibly made to compromised charmers. I defy even a
master of morbid observation to perambulate New York
unless he be interested; so that in a case of memories so
gathered the interest must be taken as a final fact. Let me
figure it, to this end, as lively in every connection—and so
indeed no more lively at one mild crisis than at another.
The crisis—even of observation at the morbid pitch—is
inevitably mild in cities intensely new; and it was with the
quite peculiarly insistent newness of the upper reaches of
the town that the spirit of romantic inquiry had always, at
the best, to reckon. There are new cities enough about the
world, goodness knows, and there are new parts enough of
old cities—for examples of which we need go no farther
than London, Paris and Rome, all of late so mercilessly
renovated. But the newness of New York—unlike even
that of Boston, I seemed to discern—had this mark of its

very own, that it affects one, in every case, as having
treated itself as still more provisional, if possible, than any
poor dear little interest of antiquity it may have annihilat-
ed. The very sign of its energy is that it doesn't believe in
itself; it fails to succeed, even at a cost of millions, in per-
suading you that it does. Its mission would appear to be,
exactly, to gild the temporary, with its gold, as many inch-
es thick as may be, and then, with a fresh shrug, a shrug
of its splendid cynicism for its freshly detected inability to
convince, give up its actual work, however exorbitant, as
the merest of stop-gaps. The difficulty with the compromised charmer is just this constant inability to convince; to
convince ever, I mean, that she is serious, serious about
any form whatever, or about anything but that perpetual
passionate pecuniary purpose which plays with all forms,
which derides and devours them, though it may pile up the
cost of them in order to rest a while, spent and haggard,
in the illusion of their finality.

The perception of this truth grows for you by your simply walking up Fifth Avenue and pausing a little in presence of certain forms, certain exorbitant structures, in
other words the elegant domiciliary, as to which the illusion of finality was within one's memory magnificent and
complete, but as to which one feels to-day that their life
wouldn't be, as against any whisper of a higher interest,
worth an hour's purchase. They sit there in the florid

majesty of the taste of their time—a light now, alas, generally clouded; and I pretend of course to speak, in alluding to them, of no individual case of danger or doom. It is only a question of that unintending and unconvincing expression of New York everywhere, as yet, on the matter of the *maintenance* of a given effect—which comes back to the general insincerity of effects, and truly even (as I have already noted) to the insincerity of the effect of the skyscrapers themselves. There results from all this—and as much where the place most smells of its millions as elsewhere—that unmistakable New York expression of unattempted, impossible maturity. The new Paris and the new Rome do at least propose, I think, to be old—one of these days; the new London even, erect as she is on leaseholds destitute of dignity, yet does, for the period, appear to believe in herself. The vice I glance at is, however, when showing, in our flagrant example, on the forehead of its victims, much more a cause for pitying than for decrying them. Again and again, in the upper reaches, you pause with that pity; you learn, on the occasion of a kindly glance up and down a quiet cross-street (there being objects and aspects in many of them appealing to kindness) that such and such a house, or a row, is "coming down"; and you gasp, in presence of the elements involved, at the strangeness of the moral so pointed. It rings out like the crack of that lash in the sky, the play of some mighty teamster's whip, which ends by affecting you as the poor New-Yorker's one association with the idea of "powers above." "No"—this is the tune to which the whip seems flourished—"there's no step at which you shall rest, no form, as I'm constantly showing you, to which, consistently with my interests, you *can*. I build you up but to tear you down, for if I were to let sentiment and sincerity once take root, were to let any tenderness of association once accumulate, or any 'love of the old' once pass unsnubbed, what would become of *us*, who have our hands on the whipstock, please? Fortunately we've learned the secret for keeping association at bay. We've learned that the great thing is not to suffer it to so much as begin. Wherever it does begin we find we're lost; but as that takes some time we get in ahead. It's the reason, if you must know, why you shall 'run,' all, without exception, to the fifty floors. We defy you even to aspire to venerate shapes so grossly constructed as the arrangement in fifty floors. You may have a feeling for keeping on with an old staircase, consecrated by the tread of generations—especially when it's 'good,' and old staircases are often so lovely; but how can you have a feeling for keeping on with an old elevator, how can you have it any more than for keeping on with an old omnibus? You'd be ashamed to venerate the arrangement in fifty floors, accordingly, even if you could; whereby, saving you any moral trouble or struggle, they are conceived and constructed—and you must do us the justice of this care for your sensibility—in a manner to put the thing out of the question. In such a manner, moreover, as that there shall be immeasurably more of them, in quantity, to tear down than of the actual past that we are now sweeping away. Wherefore we shall be kept in precious practice. The word will perhaps be then—who knows?— for building from the earth-surface downwards; in which case it will be a question of tearing, so to speak, 'up.' It little matters, so long as we blight the superstition of rest."

Yet even in the midst of this vision of eternal waste, of conscious, sentient-looking houses and rows, full sections of streets, to which the rich taste of history is forbidden even while their fresh young lips are just touching the cup, something charmingly done, here and there, some bid for the ampler permanence, seems to say to you that the particular place only asks, as a human home, to lead the life it has begun, only asks to enfold generations and gather in traditions, to show itself capable of growing up to character and authority. Houses of the best taste are like clothes of the best tailors—it takes their age to show us how good they are; and I frequently recognized, in the region of the upper reaches, this direct appeal of the individual case of happy construction. Construction at large abounds in the upper reaches, construction indescribably precipitate and elaborate—the latter fact about it always so oddly hand in

hand with the former; and we should exceed in saying that
felicity is always its mark. But some highly liberal, some
extravagant intention almost always is, and we meet here
even that happy accident, already encountered and
acclaimed, in its few examples, down-town, of the object
shining almost absurdly in the light of its merely comparative distinction. All but lost in the welter of instances of
sham refinement, the shy little case of real refinement
detaches itself ridiculously, as being (like the saved City
Hall, or like the pleasant old garden-walled house on the
northwest corner of Washington Square and Fifth Avenue)
of so beneficent an admonition as to show, relatively speaking, for priceless. These things, which I may not take time
to pick out, are the salt that saves, and it is enough to say
for their delicacy that they are the direct counterpart of
those other dreadful presences, looming round them, which
embody the imagination of new kinds and new clustered,
emphasized quantities of vulgarity. To recall these fine notes
and these loud ones, the whole play of wealth and energy
and untutored liberty, of the movement of a breathless civilization reflected, as brick and stone and marble may
reflect, through all the contrasts of prodigious flight and
portentous stumble, is to acknowledge, positively, that one's
rambles were delightful, and that the district abutting on
the east side of the Park, in particular, never engaged my
attention without, by the same stroke, making the social

91

question dance before it in a hundred interesting forms.

The social question quite fills the air, in New York, for any spectator whose impressions at all follow themselves up; it wears, at any rate, in what I have called the upper reaches, the perpetual strange appearance as of Property perched high aloft and yet itself looking about, all ruefully, in the wonder of what it is exactly doing there. We see it perched, assuredly, in other and older cities, other and older social orders; but it strikes us in those situations as knowing a little more where it is. It strikes us as knowing how it has got up and why it must, infallibly, stay up; it has not the frightened look, measuring the spaces around, of a small child set on a mantel-shelf and about to cry out. If old societies are interesting, however, I am far from thinking that young ones may not be more so—with their collective countenance so much more presented, precisely, to observation, as by their artless need to get themselves explained. The American world produces almost every-where the impression of appealing to any attested interest for the word, the *fin mot*, of what it may mean; but I some-how see those parts of it most at a loss that are already explained not a little by the ample possession of money. This is the amiable side there of the large developments of private ease in general—the amiable side of those numerous groups that are rich enough and, in the happy vulgar phrase, bloated enough, to be candidates for the classic imputation of haughtiness. The amiability proceeds from an essential vagueness; whereas real haughtiness is never vague about itself—it is only vague about others. That is the human note in the huge American rattle of gold—so far as the "social" field is the scene of the rattle. The "business" field is a different matter—as to which the determination of the audibility in it of the human note (so interesting to try for if one had but the warrant) is a line of research closed to me, alas, by my fatally uninitiated state. My point is, at all events, that you cannot be "hard," really, with any society that affects you as ready to learn from you, and from this resource for it of your detachment combining with your proximity, what in the name of all its possessions and all its destitutions it would honestly be "at."

List of Illustrations

Page 37—TRINITY CHURCH. *Harper's Weekly*. Vol LIII. May 8, 1909. The church was established on land granted by Queen Anne in 1705. The current church is the third on this site.

Page 55—NORTHSIDE OF WASHINGTON SQUARE PARK. Unidentified photographer, c. 1910. From the Collection of The New-York Historical Society. This view shows the Washington Arch and the Church of the Ascension on Fifth Avenue.

Pge 67—CITY HALL, NEW YORK, 1900. *Harper's New Monthly Magazine*. Vol. C. April 1900. Designed by John McComb Jr. and Joseph Mangin, City Hall was built between 1803 and 1812. At that time, no one expected the city to extend beyond Chambers Street.

Page 70—MAIN FOYER—WALDORF-ASTORIA HOTEL. Unidentified photographer, c. 1903. Collection of The New-York Historical Society. The original site of this hotel was on Fifth Avenue and 34th Street, where the Empire State Building now stands.

Page 85—A CITY IN A STREET—NASSAU STREET IN LOWER NEW YORK. Drawn by Vernon Howe Bailey. *Harper's Weekly*. Vol. LII. April 4, 1908. The bustling financial and commercial center around Wall Street was well established by the time James visited it in 1904.